FJH PIANO TEACHING LIBRARY

Jewish Festival and Folk Songs

BOOK TWO

ELEMENTARY/LATE ELEMENTARY

**Compiled and arranged by
Renée and David Karp**

**THE
F·J·H
MUSIC
COMPANY
INC.**

Frank J. Hackinson

Production: Frank J. Hackinson
Production Coordinator: Satish Bhakta
Editor: Edwin McLean
Engraving: Tempo Music Press, Inc.
Printer: Tempo Music Press, Inc.

ISBN-13: 978-1-56939-676-6

The songs in this collection represent a cross-section of some of the best-known Hebrew melodies. Arranged especially for upper elementary-level pianists, these arrangements may be played and enjoyed by anyone interested in exploring Hebrew music. The teacher accompaniments may be used for enhancing lesson material or for duet performance in recitals. We hope that you have as much enjoyment and fun in playing and singing these songs as we've had in preparing them for you.

Renée and David Karp

Pronunciation Guide

Every language has its special sounds. The following guide will help you in pronouncing the Hebrew words in this collection.

a	as in *mama*
e	as in *bet*
eh	as in *bet, used only at the end of the word*
i	as in *sit* or *bring*
o	as in *softer* or *some* and sometimes long o as in *home*
u	as in *cool* or *rule*
oi	as in *foil*
ei	as in *veil*
g	as in *got* (hard g)
ch	as in *Bach*

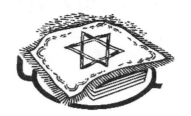

CONTENTS

This book is dedicated to Macy Golman, Jed Golman, Grey Golman, Shira Karp, Eli Karp, and Max Karp—they enhance and give special meaning to our holiday celebrations.

My Dreidel

A dreidel is a top that has four letters, one on each side. The letters mean "a great miracle happened there."
Children play games with their dreidels during the eight days of Chanukah.

Traditional
Arr. David Karp

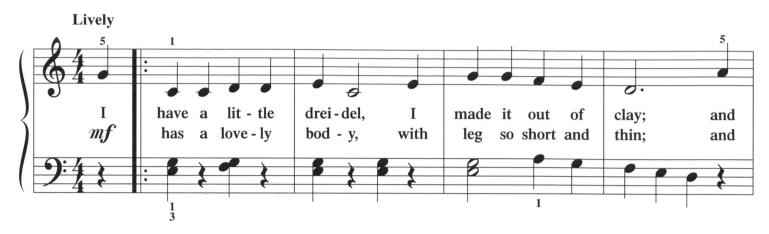

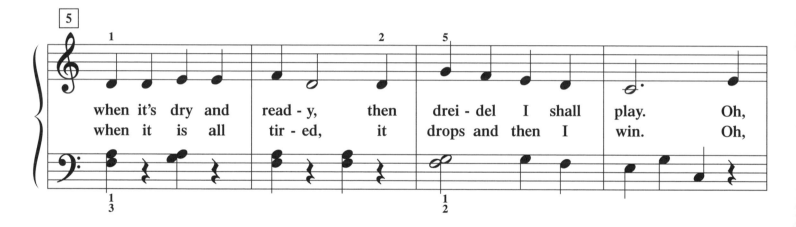

Teacher Duet: (Student plays 1 octave higher)

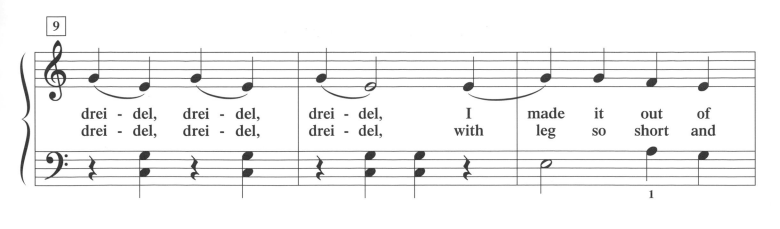

drei - del, drei - del, drei - del, I made it out of
drei - del, drei - del, drei - del, with leg so short and

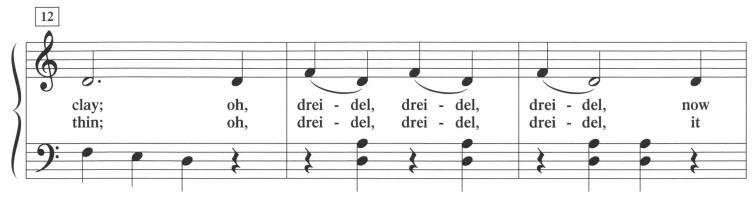

clay; oh, drei - del, drei - del, drei - del, now
thin; oh, drei - del, drei - del, drei - del, it

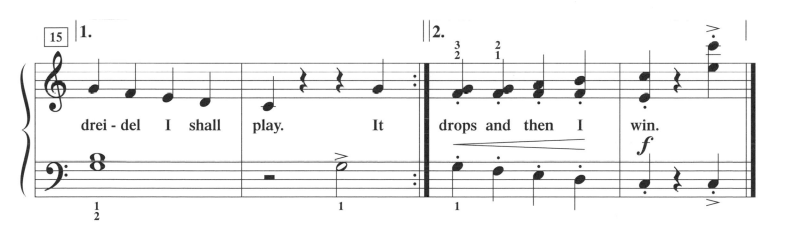

1. drei - del I shall play. It   **2.** drops and then I win.

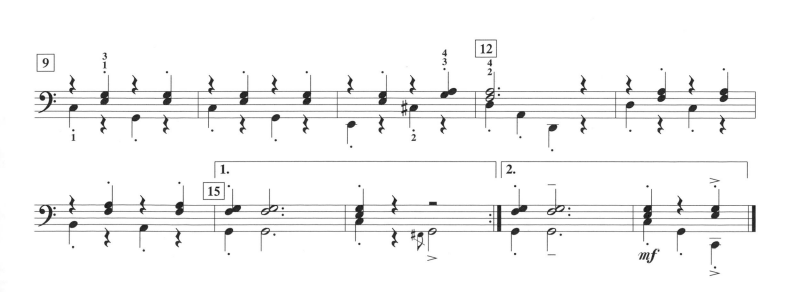

How Many Candles

We celebrate the eight nights of Chanukah by lighting a Chanukiah—a nine-candle menorah.
On the first night, we light two candles. We light a server candle called the Shamash.
We use the Shamash candle to light the first candle. On the second night we light the Shamash,
which is used to light two candles. We add a candle each night for eight nights.

Words and Music: Jackie Cytrynbaum
Arr. David Karp

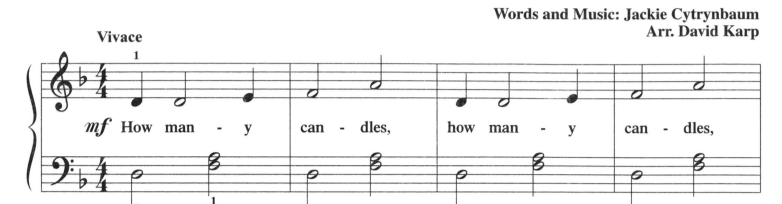

mf How man - y can - dles, how man - y can - dles,

how man - y can - dles do we light

Teacher Duet: (Student plays 1 octave higher)

Chanukah

This song tells us about the spinning of dreidels during Chanukah.

Traditional
Arr. David Karp

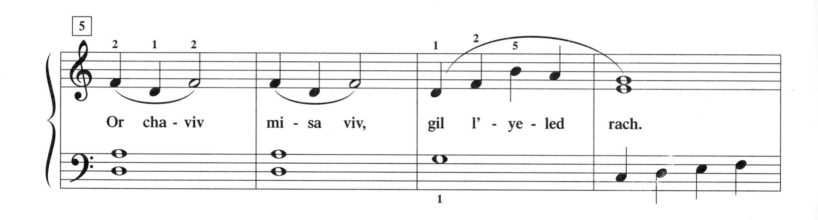

Teacher Duet: (Student plays 1 octave higher)

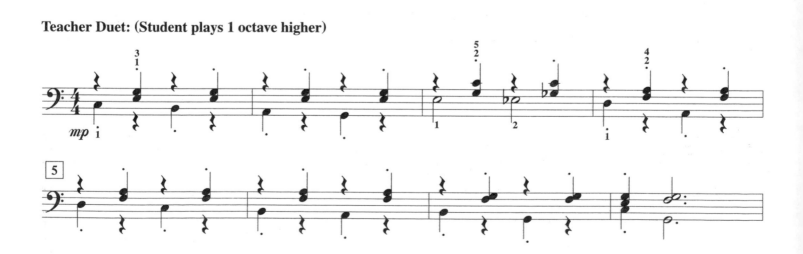

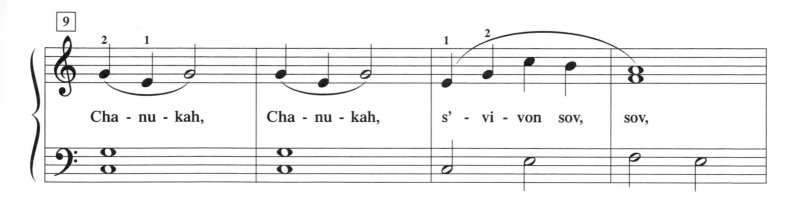

Cha - nu - kah,   Cha - nu - kah,   s' - vi - von sov,   sov,

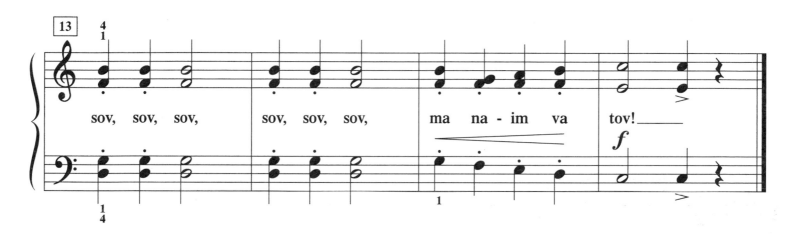

sov, sov, sov,   sov, sov, sov,   ma na - im va tov!

Translation:
Chanukah, Chanukah is such a beautiful holiday;
Lovely light all around brings joy to children.
Chanukah, Chanukah; turn, turn the dreidel.
Turn, turn, turn; turn, turn, turn;
What a pleasure and delight!

Rock of Ages
(Ma'oz Tzur)

This song tells of the many times Israel struggled to be free. It tells how the Jewish people
stayed strong because they believed in God. This song is sung after kindling the Chanukah lights.

Traditional
Arr. David Karp

Rock of A - ges, let our song,___ Praise Thy sav - ing___ pow - er,
Ma - oz tzur ye - shu - a - ti, l' - cha na - e l - sha - bei - ach.

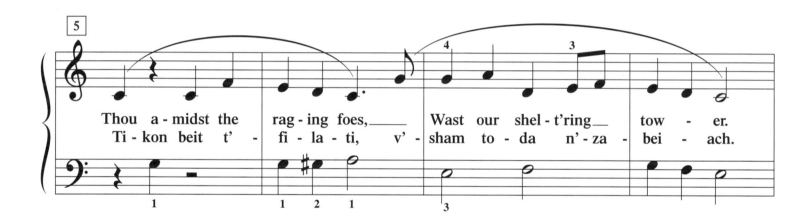

Thou a - midst the rag - ing foes,___ Wast our shel - t'ring___ tow - er.
Ti - kon beit t' - fi - la - ti, v' - sham to - da n' - za - bei - ach.

Teacher Duet: (Student plays 1 octave higher)

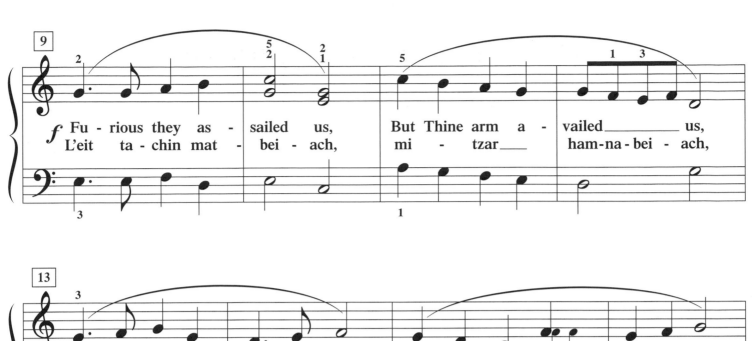

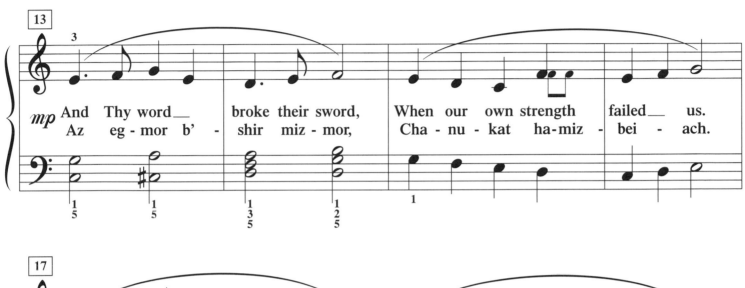

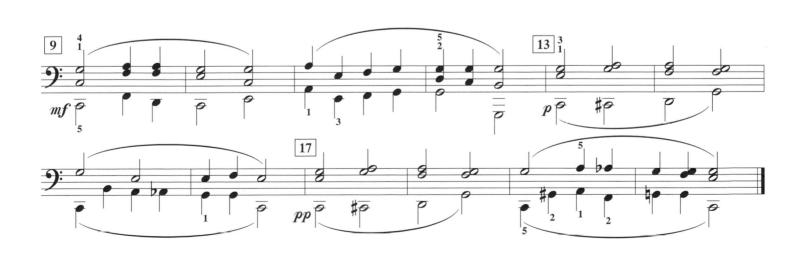

O Chanukah, O Chanukah

Lighting the menorah, playing with dreidels, and eating latkes (potato pancakes)
are some of the things that make Chanukah a fun festival.

Traditional
Arr. David Karp

mp O Cha-nu-kah, O Cha-nu-kah, come light the me - no - rah!

Let's have a par-ty, we'll all dance the ho-ra.

Teacher Duet: (Student plays 1 octave higher)

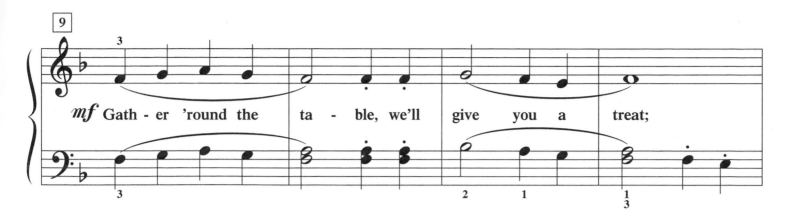

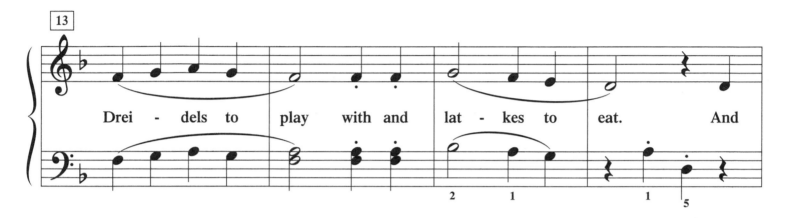

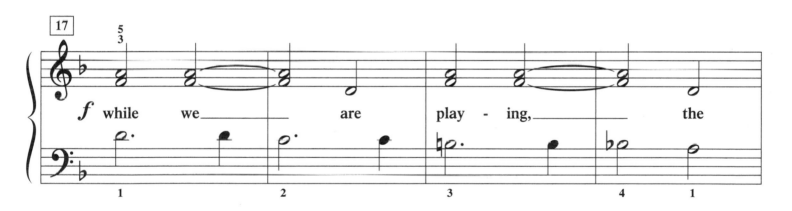

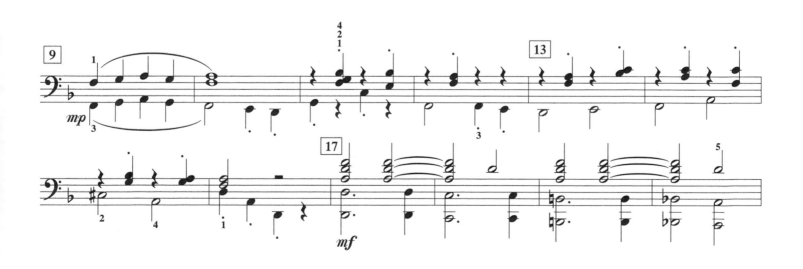

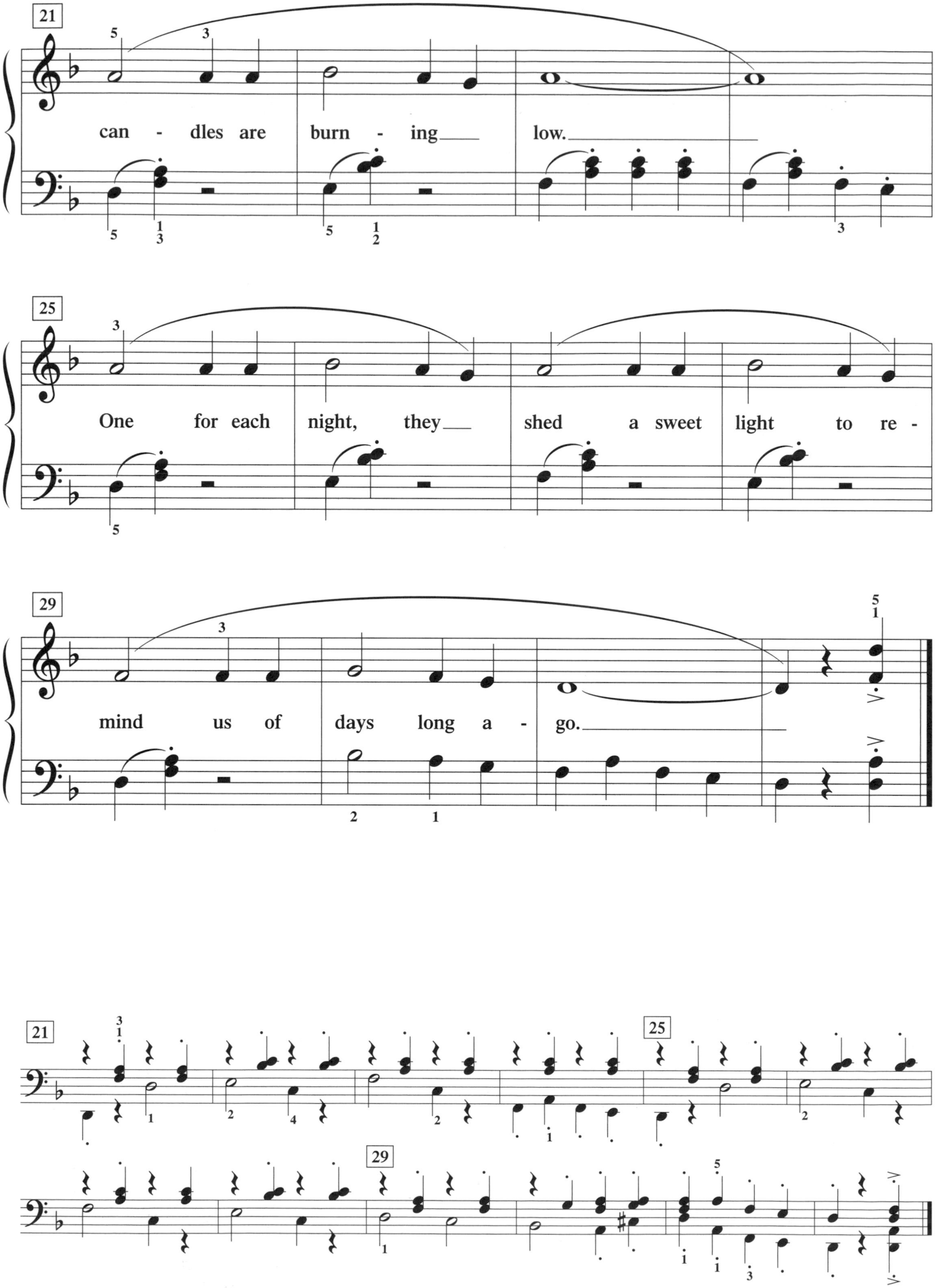
21
can - dles are burn - ing low.
25
One for each night, they shed a sweet light to re -
29
mind us of days long a - go.
21
25
29

"*My name is Max Karp and I am five years old. I like to go to my grandparents house for Chanukah. My cousins and I spin dreidels. We give and get presents, that's a lot of fun.*"

Dayeinu

This song is sung during the Passover Seder and tells of the many wonderful things God did for the Jewish people.
They are grateful for all these things, saying that just one of them would have been enough.

Traditional
Arr. David Karp

Brightly

Teacher Duet: (Student plays 1 octave higher)

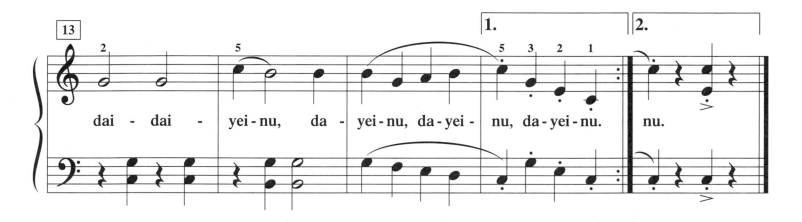

Additional verses:

2. I-lu na-tan, na-tan la-nu, na-tan la-nu et-ha Sha-bat
   Na-tan la-nu et-ha Sha-bat Da-yei-nu. (Chorus)

3. I-lu na-tan, na-tan la-nu, na-tan la-nu et-ha To-rah
   Na-tan la-nu et-ha To-rah Da-yei-nu. (Chorus)

Translation:
1. Had God brought us forth from Egypt, it would have been enough.
2. Had God given us the Sabbath, it would have been enough.
3. Had God given us the Torah, it would have been enough.

Ma Nishtana?

The Passover Seder usually takes place in the home. The Four Questions are asked by the youngest child.
These questions are answered explaining the history of this spring festival of freedom.

Traditional
Arr. David Karp

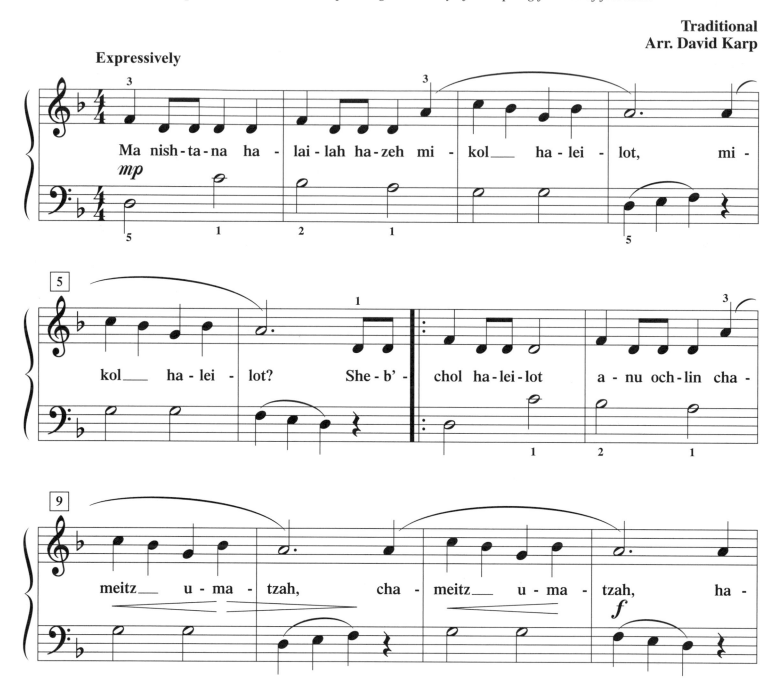

Teacher Duet: (Student plays 1 octave higher)

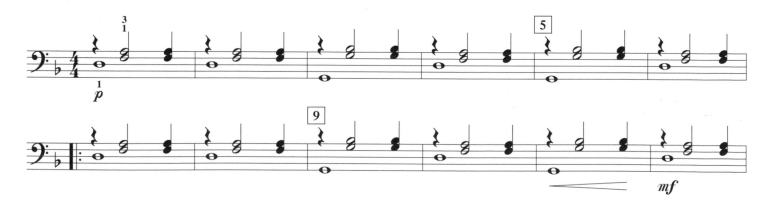

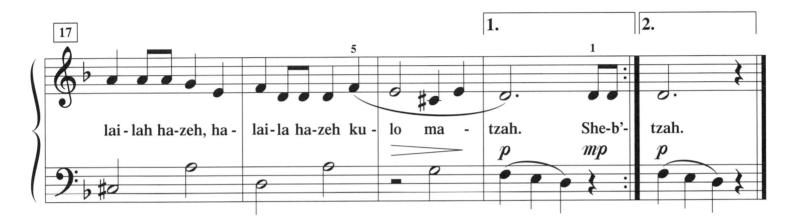

Additional verses:

2. She-b'chol ha-lei-lot, a-nu och-lin, sh-ar y-ra-kot, sh-ar y-ra-kot,
   Ha-lai-lah ha-zeh, ha-lai-lah ha-zeh, ku-lo ma-ror,
   Ha-lai-lah ha-zeh, ha-lai-lah ha-zeh, ku-lo ma-ror.

3. She-b'chol ha-lei-lot, ein-a-nu, mat-bi-lin a-fi-lu pa-am e-chat, mat-bi-lin a-fi-lu pa-am e-chat,
   Ha-lai-lah ha-zeh, ha-lai-lah ha-zeh, sh-tei p-a-mim,
   Ha-lai-lah ha-zeh, ha-lai-lah ha-zeh, sh-tei p-a-mim.

4. She-b'chol ha-lei-lot, a-nu och-lin, bein yosh-vin u-vein m'su-bin, bein yosh-vin u-vein m'su-bin,
   Ha-lai-lah ha-zeh, ha-lai-lah ha-zeh, ku-la-nu m'-su-bin,
   Ha-lai-lah ha-zeh, ha-lai-lah ha-zeh, ku-la-nu m'-su-bin.

Translation:

Why is this night different from all other nights?
On other nights we eat either leavened bread or matzah; on this night only matzah.
On all other nights we eat all kinds of herbs; on this night we eat bitter herbs.
On all other nights we do not dip herbs at all; on this night we dip them twice.
On all other nights we eat in an ordinary manner; tonight we eat with a special ceremony.

"My name is Shira Micol Karp. I am eight years old and I like Passover because we get to be with family. I think it is cool to be with family and also give and receive gifts during the holiday. It's fun because we search for the Afikomen (hidden matzah). If I find it I like it because I get a special prize. I also like to fill up the glass of wine for Elijah the Prophet. I know that Elijah is at the house by the way the glass shakes."

Ani Purim

This joyous song tells about the festive holiday of Purim.

Traditional
Arr. David Karp

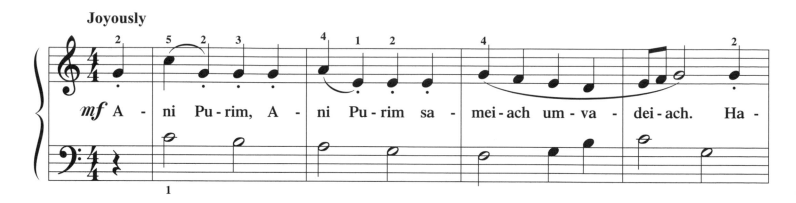

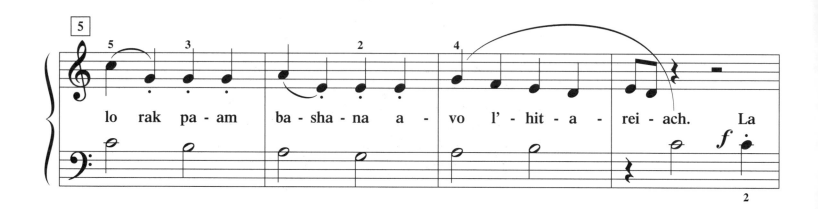

Teacher Duet: (Student plays 1 octave higher)

Translation:
I am Purim. Although I visit but once a year, I am a welcome guest.

Chag Purim

*Purim is a day to be happy. There is lots of noisemaking, costume wearing, and fun. The noisemaker (gragger)
is used to drown out the name of Haman—the man who tried to destroy the Jews—during the reading
of the Book of Esther (Megillah).*

Traditional
Arr. David Karp

Chag Pu - rim, Chag Pu - rim, Chag ga - dol hu la - y'hu - dim.

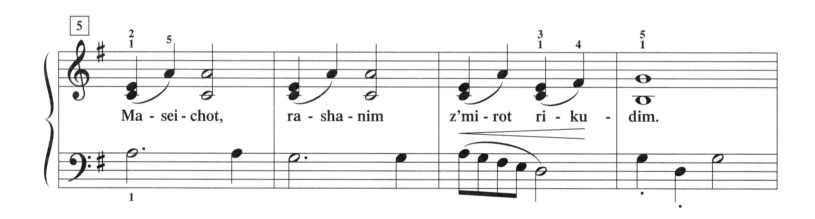

Ma - sei - chot, ra - sha - nim z'mi - rot ri - ku - dim.

Teacher Duet: (Student plays 1 octave higher)

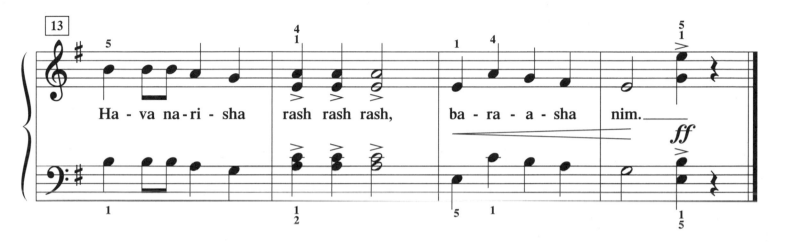

Translation:
Purim is a festive holiday for the Jewish people. There are masks, noisemakers (graggers), songs, and dances. Let us make noise with the noisemakers (graggers).

Haman, a Wicked Man

When a People is saved from being hurt, merry-making takes place.
The defeat of the evil Haman is the theme of this joyful tune.

Traditional
Arr. David Karp

Lyrics: 1. Oh, once there was a wick-ed, wick-ed man, and Ha-man was his name, Sir. He lied and lied a-bout the Jews, though they were not to blame, Sir.

Chorus: Oh, to-day we'll mer-ry, mer-ry be;

Teacher Duet: (Student plays 1 octave higher)

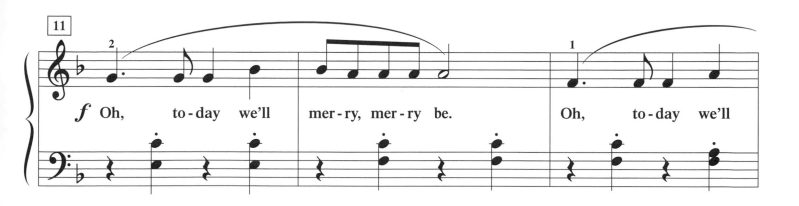

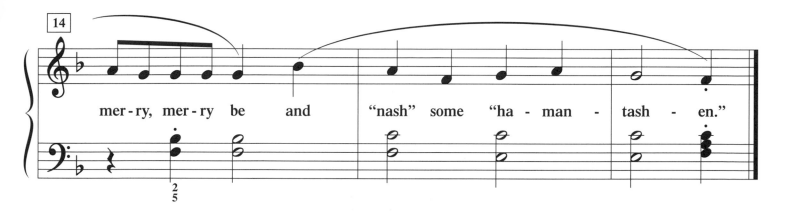

Additional verses:

2. And Esther was the lovely queen of King Ahasuerus,
   When Haman said he'd squelch us all, oh my how he did scare us.
   (Chorus)

3, But Mordecai, her cousin bold, said, "What a dreadful villain!
   If we don't act at once, my dear, our life's not worth a shilling."
   (Chorus)

4. When Esther, speaking to the King of Haman's plot, made mention,
   "Ha ha!" said he, "Oh no he won't; I'll spoil his bad intention."
   (Chorus)

5. And so, my friend, came to an end this clever Mister Smarty,
   For he became a wiser man at Esther's little party.
   (Chorus)

Zum Gali Gali

For the pioneers of Israel, working on the land was a dream come true.

Traditional
Arr. David Karp

Teacher Duet: (Student plays 1 octave higher)

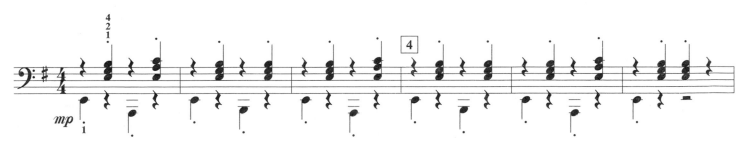

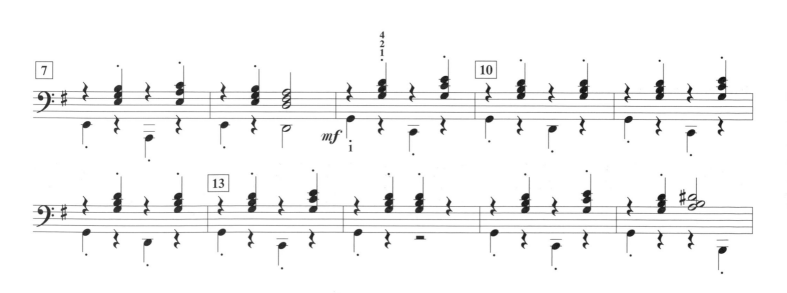

Adon Olam

This is one of the best-known Jewish songs. For the past 600 years it has been included in the prayerbook.
There are many melodies for this song. This is one of the favorites.

Traditional
Arr. David Karp

Lyrics: A - don O - lam a - sher - ma - lach B' - te - rem kol ye - tsir niv - ra Le eit na - a sa, v' - chef - tso kol, a - zai me - lech she - mo nik - ra V' - a - cha - rei, kich -

Teacher Duet: (Student plays 1 octave higher)

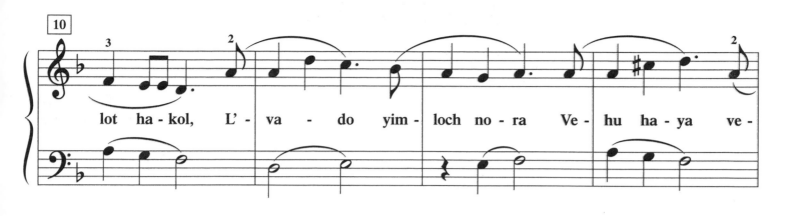

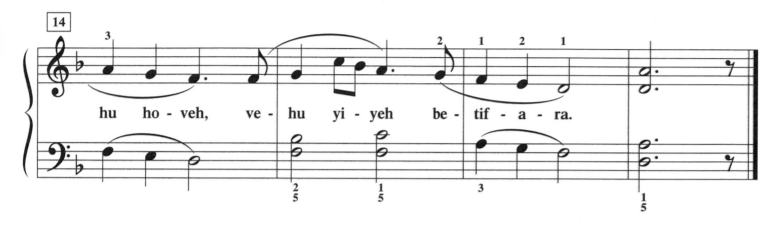

Additional verse:
Ve-hu e-chad ve-ein shei-ni, le-ham-shil lo le-hach-bi-ra
Be-li rei-shit be-li tach-lit, ve-lo ha-oz ve-ha-mis-ra.
Ve-hu ei-li, ve-chai go-a-li, ve-tsur chev-li be-eit tsa-ra
Ve-hu ni-si u-ma-nos li me nat ko-si be-yom ek-ra.

Be-ya-do, af-kid ru-chi, be-eit i-shan ve-a-i-ra
Ve-im ru-chi ge-vi-ya-ti, A-do-nai li ve-lo i-ra.

Hinei Ma Tov

This song comes from Psalm 133. The idea of brotherly love is a very important one for the Jewish people.

Traditional
Arr. David Karp

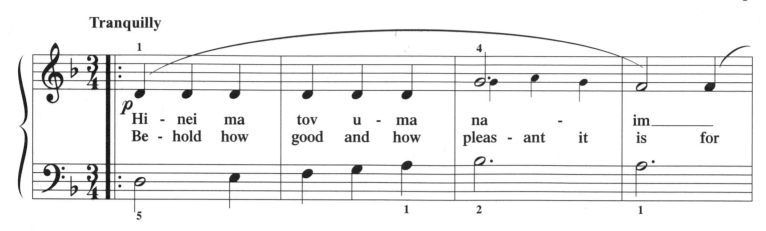

Teacher Duet: (Student plays 1 octave higher)

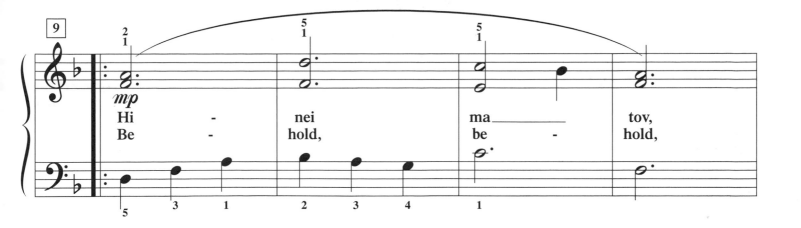

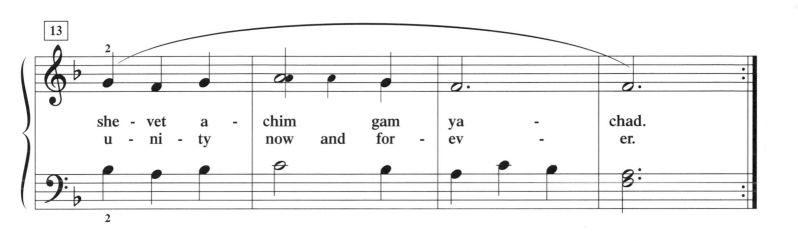

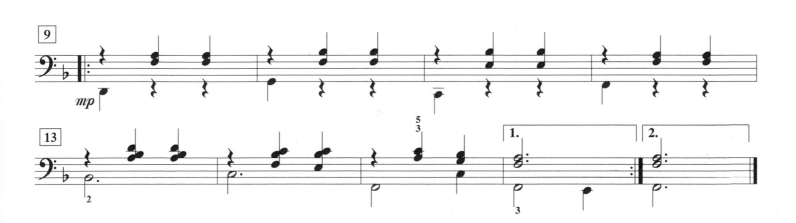

Hava Nagila

Happy occasions call for singing and dancing.
This song is one of the most popular folk songs.

Traditional
Arr. David Karp

Teacher Duet: (Student plays 1 octave higher)

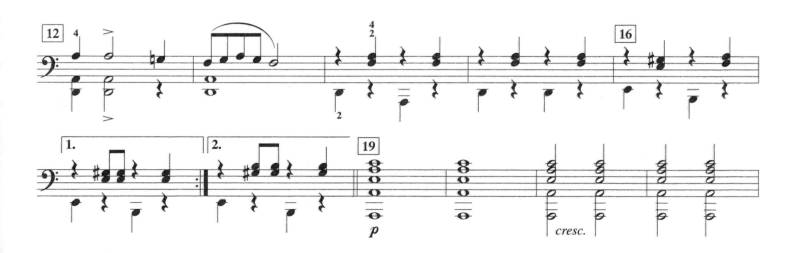

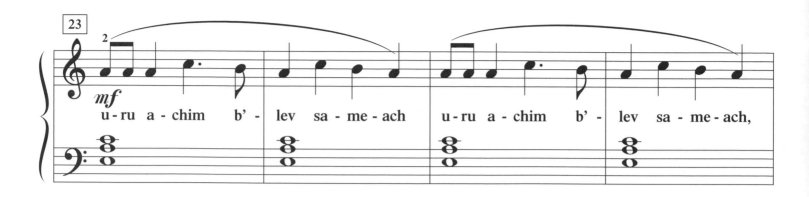

Translation:
Come let us rejoice and be glad.
Let us shout for joy and be glad.
Awake, brothers and sisters,
Arise with a joyful heart!

Raisins and Almonds

This lovely Yiddish lullaby speaks of the simple things in life: raisins, almonds, and honey.
Yiddish is a language that was spoken by many Jews in Europe.

Abraham Goldfaden
Arr. David Karp

Teacher Duet: (Student plays 1 octave higher)

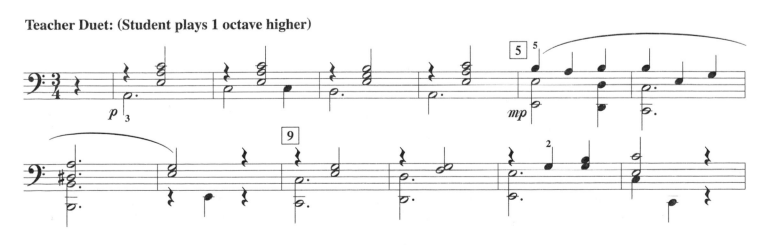

FJH1734

Hatikva

Natali Herz Imber (1856-1911) wrote this poem that was published in a collection called
"Barkai" (Jerusalem, 1886). "Hatikva" became the national anthem of the State of Israel.

Traditional
Arr. David Karp

Andante con moto

Kol__ od ba-lei vav   p'ni - ma.   Ne - fesh Ye-hu - di   ho - mi - yah.   Ul

fa - a - tei__ miz - rach,   ka - di - ma.   A - yin l'-Tzi - yon   tzo - fi - ya.

Teacher Duet: (Student plays 1 octave higher)

Sh'ma Yisrael

The Shema is often called the "watchword of our faith" by Jews.
It is an important part of the Jewish worship service.

Traditional
Arr. David Karp

Translation:
Hear, O Israel: the Lord is our God, the Lord is One!
Blessed is His glorious kingdom forever and ever.

Teacher Duet: (Student plays 1 octave higher)

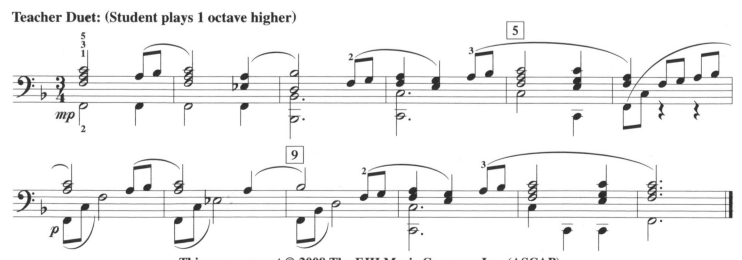